THREE NOVELS

Also by Elizabeth Robinson

Also Known As, Apogee, 2009

The Orphan and Its Relations, Fence, 2008

Under That Silky Roof, Burning Deck, 2006

Apostrophe, Apogee, 2006

Apprehend, Fence & Apogee, 2004

Pure Descent, Sun & Moon, 2003

Harrow, Omnidawn, 2001

House Made of Silver, Kelsey Street, 2000

Bed of Lists, Kelsey Street, 1990

In the Sequence of Falling Things, Paradigm, 1990

THREE NOVELS

HOMAGE TO WILKIE COLLINS AND GEORGE GISSING

Elizabeth Robinson

OMNIDAWN PUBLISHING

RICHMOND, CALIFORNIA

2011

Cover art: Fran Herndon, Quilt, 6'7" x 5"3", percale cotton and gabardine.

Courtesy of artist.

Book cover and interior design by Cassandra Smith

Library of Congress Catalog-in-Publication Data

Robinson, Elizabeth, 1961-
Three novels : homage to Wilkie Collins and George Gissing / Elizabeth Robinson.
    p. cm.
Poems.
ISBN 978-1-890650-51-3 (pbk. : alk. paper)
I. Title. II. Title: Homage to Wilkie Collins and George Gissing.
PS3568.O2883T57 2011
811'.54--dc22

                    2011026814

Published by Omnidawn Publishing, Richmond, California

www.omnidawn.com   (510) 237-5472   (800) 792-4957

10 9 8 7 6 5 4 3 2 1

ISBN: 978-1-890650-51-3

Acknowledgements:

Some of these poems, or parts thereof have appeared in *Conjunctions*,
Web Conjunctions, *Connotation Press*, *Monkey Puzzle*, *The New
Review*, and *Shearsman*.

I also wish to express my appreciation of Kate Summerscale's *The Suspicions
of Mr. Whicher* (New York: Walker & Company, 2008) which informed my
poem, "The Moonstone."

A million thanks and always much love to Rusty Morrison and Brian Teare
for insightful editorial response and advice.

To the memory of my father,
Bruce C. Robinson,
who first introduced me to these novels.

BOOK ONE:

THE MOONSTONE

Origin Myth

It has been said that the detective story has structural elegance because it begins with a murder and unravels neatly backwards to relate the cause of the murder: a solution. But this was not true of the first detective story. That story entailed no murders, only a loss, various losses.

Eventually a death. In truth, more than one death. And a murder after all.

Disguise

One body fits inside another body, like a turban upon a head. The role of disguise comes here to constitute itself as clairvoyant. Little niggling itch between the one and the other. The costumed fellow is a juggler who juggles his selfhood like so many balls. We expend energy to recognize whom, it may be, is the villain. Or the hero. Why one narrator becomes the butler, telling us to whom we should direct our solicitations. Another is the evangelist, leaving tracts as clues. As though the butler knows whom it is he serves. Look this way, he says. Or he omits to mention the travelling performers, their more overt disguise, an opacity on top of the curse.

Decorum

One wishes the surface were as pleasant to the finger as it is to the eye.

Perhaps one can never touch it.

Perhaps one is touched too much.

She was ugly. She was beautiful. Her appearance was altered.

One shoulder was raised above another and made of her a freak. Or her

lovely lips were compressed and drained of color. Always to be called lesser.

In a realm in which one's reason is continually partaken of and one's reason

is ever mottled with skepticism. Just as the surface is mottled with secrets.

Look how the feminine boot print leads to the shore and not back from

it. How the landscape shimmies with this tide. Alas, the shore is soaked

through and through with what one knows but does not tell, the courtesy

of it, as it turns to quicksand—receptive, that is, to the weight of the visitor,

blurring the footprint politely as it harries the rain.

The Nightshirt

Contemporary history reveals that outside our fiction there was another shirt, and it, too, stained—but with blood. This narrative's dilution turns blood to paint. Both garments have since disappeared, and so history also gives way to fiction. The laundry books insist that these garments were real, making the record of this record the least of our fictions. In other words, these are the accounts most accurate to the invention.

Revisit

The theory has changed while the theorist whistles. Even God can repent of his actions, yes? It appears that the thief steals only from the thief, and so much harder to apprehend. The detective would have us pull up the gravel path and instead lay down a lush turf that will compromise all surfaces. Yes, the surface quavers, but only at that periphery, that shore beyond which we are hard pressed to see.

Quicksand

Remark how, granular and precise, the sand is suffused with tidewater. How the quality of the material is altered by its encounter with the liquid we call "sea." One struggles to refrain from aesthetic judgment. What one party calls grotesque, an impropriety of nature, another admires. Where we exercised the restraint called "survival," she relinquished that desire for another.

Clairvoyance

The boy pours drops of ink on his palm where it spreads as a map, telling by its traverse where the great jewel has gone. "Regent of the night": moon. The moonstone glowing toward the language of its own retrieval. Others equate the map with the blindfold, attributing its efficacy to the superstition of sex, of race, "what no practical man can believe." Not truth.

Surface

Clairvoyance, too, bears some relation to the surface. To see thus: flying as the crow flies. So one is enabled to make mere surface out of indisposition. And arrive. One need not embroider the fabric, nor even sew its panels together, for the eye flies as a veil over the body, never immodest, but simply in true relation to truth.

Each party pauses, moving away from the object of its desire, and so the terrain is clarified.

Each narrator makes tensile the cordage that marks his or her terrain, and from above, the eye cannot help but note the pretty pattern that stands out in their overlap. It remains nonetheless a barren site.

Clairvoyance would appall the truth by refusing to keep its secrets. The eye flies over the naked body, yes, but sees only skin. Sees the forms of travel, the formula partaken of by those who attempt to escape.

Clairvoyance, then, as a sense of humor, its own map.

That is,

the ability to read the skin, its legend of flush and pallor. The true body, the one which, despite all its acumen, cannot get away.

A Danger to Oneself

The first of the fallen is now gone. She is regretted. By many versions she secreted herself, by many avenues was hidden. A missive. A length of chain. A refusal to make known. The soothsayer, our 'genius,' apparently designated her the villain when the greatest obstacle was her innocence. By which I mean the manner in which she departed the world of firm outline and forced herself into formlessness.

As Predicted

Within three days, all that the oracle, that supreme rationalist, had predicted did indeed transpire. One can only rejoin to his self-assurance that this solves nothing, discloses nothing. All the potentially guilty parties depart, all at reverses, one with the other. Which eventuality might just as easily have been predicted as a crease in the map which obscures the vital turn-off from the road.

Sleepwalking

The idea is to reenact what you did, but cannot recollect that you have done. The purpose is to walk over the very surface of sleep, as Christ walked over the surface of the water.

And all along, riptide and quicksand hissing through the windows.

The physician promises a form of restitution and this he offers by way of smoothing the text that covers the page. He does this with his own speculative interpolations. He offers that he will soon die and so is at liberty to experiment freely.

Soon you will be walking in the dark, buoyant upon it.

Soon you will relinquish the habits that consoled you. No matter that they filled your lungs, but the breath, too, is just a taste of the façade that fronts the atmosphere.

The physician offers you a means of relinquishing the guilt that has been your enduring companion. To do so, you must once again smudge the white fabric of your shift, disrupt the paint that would have covered the threshold.

Who is it that levitates over the tide as the savior is reported to have done, who dwindles in consciousness, as though slumber's helium could loft the perpetrator over pain?

Blame

The recumbent body is our model for blame. The waking mind uses this plane as a promenade. The dreamer asks the dream for its counsel and is misled. Fault sleepwalks. Oh phantom. Oh witness, how you multiply. The sleepers unite in their helplessness before what they know. The soft, mathematical breath of nocturne. The fresh paint on the doorsill clings to the nightclothes of this apparition. Blame's synonym would be guilt, oblivious of itself, yet tinting the garment. Supine as the hour, guilt flattened in the insomniac's eye.

Pariah

Think of the self as a locket in which one must carry something foul: a secret innocence. One outcast strolls with another along the country road where they share confidences. A third, the party whose memory has been ruined by his own illness, imparts vindication in fragments and from a distance. This is experimental theory: piecemeal, made of an unconvincing rationality. The culprits are not really culprits. Yet in the eyes of the world, vindication bears little relation to mercy.

Jewel

The gem is the unfaithful consort. Even when its theft is replicated, the jewel itself is not in attendance. Such surface or depth, by refracting light, implants a curse on the eye that uses it as lens. Any object that promises such transparency must eventually be abducted because of its role as actor: purely baroque. Any seeming clarity betrays the ornamentation of the body that would clasp it, wear it on its bosom.

Laudanum

One wishes for the opiate bequeathed by virtue, but even minor players in the story admit that scandal has a way of dogging, of clinging to one's clothing like stale smoke. Against that faint stink, one struggles to no effect. We like our propriety. One can "set one's affairs in order," but this too is a sedative, not an activity but a means of avoidance. Rather the active duplicity: the physician who sneaks narcotic drops into the drinking glass so that the protagonist, whomever he or she may be, believes they sleep naturally.

Decorum

Our decorum is happiness deferred. Our coastline is unsteady. Decorum is *of* the beloved, in transit *around* the beloved. Stealthier, this, than actual pursuit.

Our witness must profess us, then die. Our adjudicator shall remove himself to exile, our servant recuse himself.

Our camouflage, our jewel, is lost to us forever. So we end. This is our troth.

As the somnambulant gropes toward the site of loss, his beloved looks on in polite and silent bliss.

BOOK TWO:

THE WOMAN IN WHITE

The pastoral

        lies diaphanous on itself

pale tissue pulled from within   There is no secrecy, only swathing—

    The consolation of the flat world

Tissue of consolation

     on the wan field   wandering

What the narrator thought was a flawless passivity

                             was not

    (Shush,

               mist)

As though it were a grand estate atop our pastoral

securing silence—

for if none are known to arrive

veiled

(rural peril)

The creature turning smoothly in its enclosure comes to

admire its own silence above all

What the narrator supposed was perfect

was the creature rapt in its white fur

struggling soundlessly in

the trap

Yet some slight disorder,

　　　　a new sequence—sister to itself

　　　　　　Did the captive creature make snow descend upon herself?

Whom did she know as her

　　　　self or pull as a thread from fabric

　　　　　　shaped from this blurred horizon—

Whose camouflage

　　　　did she wed or disclose in white weather?

From within the snare she sees the field sheared

　　　　and bleached, nude or unfinished

Hence the field

makes white snow to fall upon itself

Blemishless

Tugged from her

roughened throat—

That asylum of the open air

smothers—

Mouth-as-lair

The white words that came from that place

rely no further victim

on their

flush

A veil whose fine mesh hemmed them

in

Terrain's flesh lovingly impounded,

beautiful field, bastardy

These many forms of seizure

Once–

and sighted again–

(Hushed)

The blanket crocheted itself over the sloping plain, and all
was woolly and opaque   Not to be perturbed   Portent's
sharp consonant softened to omen

Muffled

In the dim plane, the blade scrapes wax away from the wick

Nicked at   Gloss   Raw skin

Shimmying flake of wax

Sheltering mid-road

on the unlikeliest portion of night

We beseech you, she sighs, to say nothing of a name

which was unknown to all

Resolutely the night itself puts on its muslin

gown,

loyal to a lost benefactress

And here, then, the peculiar   indirection

A simple cry

or   relative wilderness

Since when does a place

matchmake with its landscape

(when a body is promised to an earthen spouse)

The stone marking the way, and not the dress, should be

virginally white

as the one besmirches the other

Something wanting, something wanting

Cognizance

made from the snarled scraps of correspondence

So it appeared that the creature escaped

       and what was a snare

    leapt away

         tame

        .

Everywhere

purity swayed

intention

so as to allay

the ivory reversal

of pursuit

      The pursuer's eloquent lie

The abductor gently pried open the creature's mouth from which he
tugged the wooly thread that paralleled her From which he took her
colorless tongue From which he took her From which he pulled an
endless length of peerless fleece From which he lay as he lied and upon
the purity of the shawl that bound her as she was From which her pure
docility became a virtue

Blushed, this organ of
fidelity

This diary

                    falls to the page which bears
                    the landscape of an unknown hand

                    The very frame signifies departure

                    Impersonation betrays the place

who

had walked down its road to find a word or a maiden

Ache's white paving posing as tame

By its adhesive relation:
kin or link
to site

Lazy burr of bee, or ewe or hare—

And so each estate is its own golden plane of daylight
left unaware, unable to make plain the difference

between safety or hazard

A page only

It hums

Here

the hunter mounting his terrain

where sway of the crushed world is its only precision

Culprit, captor, cataloguer of passion:
cannot chase a circle

Love's catalyst
hence is
the crashing of layers,
one impressing another

The object is scoured of defining characteristics

   Fugitive

We see her only from behind and she is all alike

Whence the plot's precipice folds over, an envelope from which

more secret still,

                    the ghost falls   Shoved

Likewise, no asylum

Treasure hidden beneath its embroidered counterpane

is a mere self

                    and foreign, she meant: self

Doubling

all undone, her

      (or her)

   white membranous rind slips

burnt away

At once the creature's pelt embraces itself and all its kind—

     The land's grace incarcerates, redoubles itself

Down the linen burrow
and into the ether

How does the hollow of the land make full its vow

The clouds filled her mouth as she spoke:

                                        no,

                                                choking

Materialized as a frail part of the body glancing backward

Like that from which she pushed herself,

pushed her feral likeness

                              Transported

another death
                    — the satin open air caught afire

          as the open shift shows the bosom,

just off-balance

                              Cheapened fabric

ignited
by any attempt to recognize

The forlorn figure
turns toward
      and turns toward inkling

              Innocent imposture

Soft
little animal,
mild pelt it once wore

       Diaphanous skeleton she lifts, to ward off the several
       blows who

constitute world, gown, and endless downy lawn

Book Three:

Romance

(after Eve's Ransom)

All life sets itself upon us like a dull, iron-colored grief,

and the discipline is

to realize that we haven't died

yet.

In the story, the protagonist has no basis for hope.

In the story, the protagonist ends with a shout of joy,

and we believe this exclamation.

Yet it is hard, very difficult, to understand from whose

point of view the story is told, to understand that neutrality

functions as sympathy.

The difficulty of understanding is so large that the character must put its hands out to hold up its head, must furrow its brow.

It must be willing to wait indefinitely.

It must be willing to misunderstand itself as a means of surviving.

It must understand that its recklessness is indeed reckless even when it is absurdly modest.

It must be able to turn itself into a different character entirely, and this trait or capability will become known as love.

The romance is full of legacies: slight, often bitter, inheritances.

A beguiling photograph in the landlady's album.   But no more specific than that.

A chance meeting on the train platform where the debtor, flush with wealth, pays off his debt to the impoverished man.

This sudden wealth.

This payment of debt is meant to humiliate the man to whom the money is owed.

The countryside undulating with industrial waste.

This life.

And so the character resolves, and so the character says, over and over:

"I am going to live."

"I am going to live."

As though he were tutoring himself in an expression from a foreign language phrasebook.

Slight tune, burble,
turbulent smallness,
lost in the strewn
landscape.
Hope, drunkenness,
and their
final, bright resolve.
Clatter, moon on
the tracks. London,
lodging, the blight of
misgiving, cracks in
city pavement, her
lovely costume. Furtive,
cost, always the tune accosted,
lover giving, clutter,
window giving out to
view, worrisome
giving way to, gratitude's
cool, its foolish
duty. Late
leave-taking, the
costume's tryst, a lady's
wan face, her glove
and her wrist. From
above, the window
final, furtive, true
to its duty, its
assignation with
eavesdropping,
along with the
cost of the meal, slight
appetite, thrummed by its
own truth.
Debt, owning
up, betrayal soon
captive. Mistress,
illumine, please, misnomer
crooned to
spellbound honor. Slight
melody asked to stay, stay on, else
the debt and debtor become confused
and from each other stray.

At the core of the story is a fundamental hollowness.

This is signified by the flatness of a photograph. That it purports to show a face.

This is signified by the pallor of the main character.

At the core of the story is a contradiction that refuses to lead the reader

to a state of resolution. The nature of the story is to generate

a tension that remains suspended over the ending, like a landscape held

over its actors: they can go nowhere.

This is signified by the lodgings of the central character: all the furnishings having been given to this person by a closest "friend." They are not of his own choosing.

This is signified by the main character's diligence and mercy. At the very end, the character throws back his head and laughs.

At the core of the story, this irritability: that it is constituted by two main characters; that by no number of concrete signifiers can the narrative unite them into one.

It would be absurd to mistake patience for dispassion.

The very idea of forgiveness is the idea of a bafflement.

The lover warns the beloved to stay at a distance for safety's sake.

The best certainty is that poverty is a form of duty, an enactment

that destroys health but upholds honor.

The characters walk independently of each other up the same street,

a tenement street, and herein lies their most acute intimacy, that

they can recognize this, and can grant that at least some of the hovels

show signs of order within, of habitation, a light seen from outside.

No gasp, cry, sob, escaped tear, sigh, betrayal of feeling.

Only the loss of color in the heroine's cheek.

No such word as distress or disappointment permitted.

Neither sorrow.

We negate these, and this is our means of making measurement.

The relative silence of colorlessness, the way the lack

plumbs a certain depth. Deficiency

sounds the dimensions of this vacant space.

How does the human soul curdle?

Perhaps by self-abduction.

The consistency of the soul loses its satin texture

when it learns options.

It may take itself away.

It may demand a ransom.

How much does a self cost?

The lady had, perhaps, kidnapped her "self."

How much ease there was in adopting the role.

How beguiling the photograph, which is the only lingering image of the tale.

Her portrait.

Meanwhile, the gentleman leafs through a book he once thought too expensive.

The color plates. A study of

architecture, that is, how structure can contain, how the structure

might develop its own beauty, even integrity. How simple

to shake her hand later at the fete, seeming

hardly ever to have known this woman at all.

Elizabeth Robinson is the author of eleven books of poetry (including *Three Novels*). Her most recent books are *The Orphan & its Relations* (Fence Books) and *Also Known As* (Apogee Press). Robinson was educated at Bard College, Brown University, and the Pacific School of Religion. She has been a winner of the National Poetry Series for *Pure Descent* and the Fence Modern Poets Prize for *Apprehend*. The recipient of grants from the Fund for Poetry and the Foundation for Contemporary Arts, Robinson has also been a MacDowell Colony Fellow. Her work has been anthologized in the *Best American Poetry* (2002) and *American Hybrid*, along with many other anthologies. Robinson has taught at the University of San Francisco, the University of Colorado, Boulder, Naropa University and the Iowa Writers' Workshop. She co-edits EtherDome Chapbooks with Colleen Lookingbill and Instance Press with Beth Anderson and Laura Sims.

Three Novels
by Elizabeth Robinson

Cover text set in Edwardian Script, Engravers LT Std, Isabella Std,
Nuptial Script and Shelley Script.
Interior text set in Bernhard Modern Std.

Book offset printed by Thomson-Shore, Inc., Dexter, Michigan
on Glatfelter Natures Natural 60# archival quality recycled paper
to the Green Press Initiative standard.

Cover art by Fran Herndon
Quilt
6'7" x 5'3", percale cotton and gabardine

Cover and interior design by Cassandra Smith.

Omnidawn Publishing
Richmond, California
2011

Ken Keegan & Rusty Morrison, Co-Publishers & Senior Editors
Cassandra Smith, Poetry Editor & Book Designer
Sara Mumolo, Poetry Editor & Poetry Features Editor
Gillian Hamel, Poetry Editor & Senior Blog Editor
Jared Alford, Facebook Editor
Peter Burghardt, Bookstore Outreach Manager
Juliana Paslay, Bookstore Outreach & Features Writer
Craig Santos Perez, Media Consultant